LoVe

This book is available for special purchases in bulk by organizations and institutions, not for resale, at special discounts. Please direct your inquiries to Random House Premium Sales, fax 212-572-4961.

Please address inquiries about electronic licensing of reference products, for use on a network or in software or on CD-ROM, to the Subsidiary Rights Department, Random House Reference, fax 212-940-7352.

Visit the Random House Reference Web site: www.randomwords.com

Typeset and printed in the United States of America.

Designed by Nora Rosansky.

Library of Congress Cataloging-in-Publication Data is available.

First Edition
0 9 8 7 6 5 4 3 2 1
October 2003

ISBN 0-375-72035-9

THE GREATEST THINGS EVER SAID

Love

Leonard Roy Frank

RANDOM HOUSE
REFERENCE

INTRODUCTION

To love or not to love, that is the question. But then what is love? Love is soul-stuff, the heart's center radiating affection to the special people in our lives. Love is the airiest and surest of facts. Although it can't be proven or quantified, love's the only thing of which there can never be too much. It's the antidote to the poisons of hatred, exploitation, and violence, and the master key that opens every unbroken lock. When given away wholeheartedly, inclusively, and unconditionally, love multiplies itself. So why not give love a chance? We've tried everything else.

I've been collecting quotations for about forty years, first in loose-leaf notebooks and then, starting in the mid-1980s, on a computer. Represented on these pages are what struck me as the most meaningful and/or delightful quotes on the subject of love I've run across during this period. Although the book is not strictly organized, I've tried to place the quotes in some semblance of order rather than haphazardly. I've used the word "love" in the sense of affection, mostly what people feel for each other or what one being feels for another being. Among the broad areas of love covered in the book are romantic love, spiritual love, and platonic love.

LOVE IS THE WILD CARD OF EXISTENCE.

Rita Mae Brown, contemporary U.S. writer and poet

Love is the strangest bird
that ever winged about the world.

Lawrence Ferlinghetti, contemporary U.S. poet

Love is the white light of emotion.

Diane Ackerman, contemporary U.S. poet and writer

LOVE IS BUT the discovery of ourselves in others, and the delight in the recognition.

Alexander Smith, Scottish poet, 1830–1867

Love is a great beautifier.

Amelia Barr, English-born U.S. writer, 1831–1919

Love is a fruit in season at all times.

Mother Teresa (Agnes Gonxha Bojaxhia), Albanian nun and missionary, 1910–1997

*L*ove is the supreme and unique law of human life, which everyone feels in the depth of one's soul.

Leo Tolstoy, Russian writer, 1828–1910
(letter to Mohandas K. Gandhi, 1910)

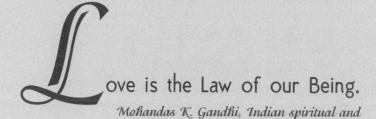

Love is the Law of our Being.

Mohandas K. Gandhi, Indian spiritual and nationalist leader, 1869–1948 (essay, 1936)

LOVE EVERYBODY AND don't let flags and religions get in the way of looking somebody in the eye and seeing the beauty of the human person.

Mairceád Corrigan, contemporary Irish peace activist

Love is what we were born with. Fear is what we learned here.

Marianne Williamson, contemporary U.S. religious figure and lecturer

There is no fear in love, but perfect love **CASTS OUT FEAR.**

John, Christian apostle, first century A.D. (1 John 4:18)

6

LOVE IS UNION WITH SOMEBODY, OR SOMETHING, outside oneself, under the condition of retaining the separateness and integrity of one's own self. It is an experience of sharing, of communing, which permits the full unfolding of one's own inner activity.

Erich Fromm, German-born U.S. psychoanalyst, 1900–1980

Love is metaphysical gravity.

R. Buckminster Fuller, U.S. architect and educator, 1895–1983

7

Love . . . binds all things together in perfect unity.
Paul, Christian apostle, first century A.D. (Colossians 3:14)

LOVE IS A STATE OF BEING IN WHICH ONE IS
AWARE OF THE UNITY OF ALL LIFE.

Richard Chamberlain, contemporary U.S. actor

*L*OVE isn't love until you give it away.

Anonymous

Love is, above all, *the gift of oneself.*

Jean Anouilh, French playwright, 1910–1987

LOVE IS THE ONE THING no one, not even God Himself, can command. It is a free gift, or it is nothing. And it is most itself, most free, when it is offered in spite of suffering, of injustice, and of death.

Archibald MacLeish, U.S. poet, 1892–1982

My love no longer depends on the way you treat me.

Rainer Maria Rilke, German poet, 1875–1926

Love makes the world go round.

Love laughs at locksmiths.

English Proverb

OLIVIA: Love sought is good, but given unsought is better.
William Shakespeare, English playwright, 1564–1616 (Twelfth Night, *1601*)

Love either finds equality or makes it.
John Dryden, English poet, 1631–1700

LOVE, SUPREME POWER OF THE HEART, MYSTE-
RIOUS ENTHUSIASM THAT ENCLOSES IN ITSELF
ALL POETRY, ALL HEROISM, ALL RELIGION!
Madame de Staël (Anne-Louise-Germaine Necker), French writer,
1766–1817

LOVE rules its kingdom without a sword.

English Proverb

Love conquers all.

Virgil, Roman poet, first century B.C.

*L*OVE understands love; it needs no talk.

Frances Ridley Havergal, English poet, 1836–1879

Love that giveth in full store
Aye receives as much, and more.

Dinah Mulock Craik, English poet and writer, 1826–1887

LOVE AND THE HOPE OF IT are not things one can learn; they are a part of life's heritage.

Maria Montessori, Italian physician and educator, 1870–1952

LOVE WOULD PUT A NEW FACE ON THIS WEARY OLD WORLD IN WHICH WE DWELL AS PAGANS AND ENEMIES TOO LONG.

Ralph Waldo Emerson, U.S. philosopher, 1803–1882

DOES my behavior in respect of love affect nothing? That is because there is not enough love in me.
Albert Schweitzer, German physician and theologian, 1875–1965

Love ... includes fellowship in suffering, in joy, and in effort.
Albert Schweitzer, German physician and theologian, 1875–1965

Love possesses not nor would it be possessed;
For love is sufficient unto love.

Kahlil Gibran, Syrian poet, 1883–1931

LOVE DOES NOT CAUSE SUFFERING: what causes it is
the sense of ownership, which is love's opposite.

Antoine de Saint-Exupéry, French aviator and writer, 1900–1944

Love is proved in the letting go.

C. Day-Lewis, Irish poet, 1904–1972

$\mathcal{L}$OVE is an act of sedition, a revolt against reason, an uprising in the body politic, a private mutiny.

Diane Ackerman, contemporary U.S. poet and writer

To love without role, without power plays, is revolution.

Rita Mae Brown, contemporary U.S. writer and poet

Love, like virtue, is its own reward.

John Vanbrugh, English playwright and architect, 1664–1726

Love has no other desire but to fulfill itself.

Kahlil Gibran, Syrian poet, 1883–1931

Love grows by service.

Charlotte Perkins Gilman, U.S. poet and writer, 1860–1935

$\mathcal{L}$OVE means not ever having to say you're sorry.
Erich Segal, contemporary U.S. writer (in the novel Love Story, *1970)*

Love, and do what you will!
St. Augustine, Christian theologian, fifth century A.D.

LOVE TRANSCENDS THE distinction between self and other. Love is the most ethically consistent experience, because selfishness and altruism no longer seem opposed or in conflict. When we rejoice in the existence of the other, his or her interests begin to approximate our own. When we promote the happiness of a loved one, we promote our own as well.

Peter R. Breggin, contemporary U.S. psychiatrist

TO LOVE IS TO TAKE DELIGHT IN THE HAPPINESS OF ANOTHER, OR, WHAT AMOUNTS TO THE SAME THING, *it is to account another's happiness as one's own.*

Gottfried Leibniz, German philosopher and mathematician, 1646–1716

21

*L*ove ... has the greatest power, and is the source of all our happiness and harmony, and makes us friends with the gods who are above us, and with one another.

Plato, Greek philosopher, fourth century B.C.

He whom love touches not
walks in darkness.

Plato, Greek philosopher, fourth century B.C.

WHAT IS LOVE? It is that powerful attraction towards all that we conceive, or fear, or hope beyond ourselves.

Percy Bysshe Shelley, English poet, 1792–1822

Familiar acts are beautiful through love.

Percy Bysshe Shelley, English poet, 1792–1822

Fate, Time, Occasion, Chance, and Change? To these
All things are subject but eternal Love.

Percy Bysshe Shelley, English poet, 1792–1822

YOU'LL NEVER BE HAPPY IF you can't figure out that loving people is all there is. And that it's more important to love than be loved. Because that is when you feel love, by loving somebody.

Gwyneth Paltrow, contemporary U.S. actor

Till I loved
I never lived Enough.

Emily Dickinson, U.S. poet,
1830–1886

That Love is all there is,
Is all we know of Love.

Emily Dickinson, U.S. poet,
1830–1886

To wait an Hour is long
If Love be just beyond
To wait Eternity is short
If Love reward the end.

Emily Dickinson, U.S. poet,
1830–1886

If I have freedom in my love,
And in my soul am free,
Angels alone that soar above
Enjoy such liberty.

Richard Lovelace, English poet,
1618–1657

Him that I love, I wish to be
Free
Even from me.

Anne Morrow Lindbergh, U.S. writer,
1906–2001

LOVE IS PERFECT IN PROPORTION TO ITS FREEDOM.

Thomas Merton, U.S. monk and writer, 1915–1968

Any great love involves sacrifice. You feel that as a father, as a husband. You give up all your freedom. But the love is so much greater than the freedom.

Nicolas Cage, contemporary U.S. actor

I SAW A WOMAN SLEEPING. In her sleep she dreamt life stood before her, and held in each hand a gift—in the one hand love, in the other freedom. And she said to the woman, "Choose." And the woman waited long: and she said, "Freedom." And life said, "Thou has well chosen. If thou hadst said 'love,' I would have given thee that thou didst ask for; and I would have gone from thee, and returned to thee no more. Now, the day will come when I shall return. On that day I shall bear both gifts in one hand." I heard the woman laugh in her sleep.

Olive Schreiner, South African writer and social critic, 1855–1910

There is no remedy for love but to love more.

Henry David Thoreau, U.S. philosopher, 1817–1862

*P*ursue some path, however narrow and crooked, in which you can walk with love and reverence.

Henry David Thoreau, U.S. philosopher, 1817–1862

THEIR LOVE IS the same for enemies and friends.

Bhagavad Gita, Hindu scriptures, sixth century B.C.

They are my true brothers because whether they see good in me or evil, *they love me still.*

St. Augustine, Christian theologian, fifth century A.D.

All people are strangers and enemies to us except those we love.

George Bernard Shaw, British playwright and critic, 1856–1950

34

WE must love one another or die.
W. H. Auden, English-born U.S. poet, 1907–1973

We must love, starting with ourselves, or die.
Alfred Kazin, U.S. literary critic, 1915–1998

WE are obliged to love one another. We are not strictly bound to "like" one another.

Thomas Merton, U.S. monk and writer, 1915–1968

If you would be loved, be worthy of being loved.

Ovid, Roman poet, first century B.C.

If you would be loved, love and be lovable.
    Benjamin Franklin, U.S. printer, inventor, and statesman,
        1706–1790

IF TO BE BELOVED BY OUR brethren be
the great object of our ambition, the surest way of obtaining it is
by our conduct to show that we really love them.
    Adam Smith, Scottish economist and philosopher, 1723–1790

37

THERE IS ONLY one happiness in life, to love and be loved.
George Sand (Armandine-Aurore-Lucile Dudevant), French writer,
1804–1876

The most vital right is the right to love and be loved.
Emma Goldman, Lithuanian-born U.S. political activist and writer,
1869–1940

THE GREATEST THING YOU'LL EVER LEARN
IS JUST TO LOVE AND BE LOVED IN RETURN.
Eden Ahbez, U.S. songwriter, 1905–1995
(in the song "Nature Boy," 1948)

38

ALL that we deeply love becomes a part of us.
Helen Keller, U.S. writer, lecturer, and educator, 1880–1968

We are what we love.
Dean William Ralph Inge, English prelate and writer, 1860–1954

A DISINTERESTED LOVE is free from hope and from fear, and from regard for personal advantage.
Gottfried Leibniz, German philosopher and mathematician, 1646–1716

The aim of love is to love: *no more, and no less.*
Oscar Wilde, English playwright, 1854–1900

Two persons love in one another the future good which they aid one another to unfold.

Margaret Fuller, U.S. writer, 1810–1850

THE proof of true love is to be unsparing in criticism.

Molière, French playwright, 1622–1673

Who loves well, corrects well.

English Proverb

Whatever is done from love
always occurs beyond good and evil.

Friedrich Nietzsche, German philosopher, 1844–1900

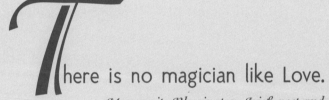

There is no magician like Love.

Marguerite Blessington, Irish poet and writer,
1789–1849

IT is not so much true that all the world loves a lover as that a lover loves all the world.

Ruth Rendell, contemporary U.S. writer

I love, and the world is mine!

Florence Earle Coates, U.S. poet, 1850–1927

JUST AS LOVE for one individual which excludes the love for others is not love, love for one's country which is not part of one's love for humanity is not love, but idolatrous worship.

Erich Fromm, German-born U.S. psychoanalyst, 1900–1980

Exclusive love is a contradiction in itself.

Erich Fromm, German-born U.S. psychoanalyst, 1900–1980

BRUTUS: Who is here so vile that will not love his country?

William Shakespeare, English playwright, 1564–1616

(Julius Caesar, 1599)

45

We forgive to the extent we love.

François de La Rochefoucauld, French writer, 1613–1680

The art of love—giving and taking become one.

Hermann Hesse, German writer, 1877–1962

The essence of love is kindness.

Robert Louis Stevenson, Scottish writer, 1850–1894

HUMAN NATURE IS so constructed that it gives affection most readily to those who seem least to demand it.

Bertrand Russell, English mathematician and philosopher,
1872–1970

Love should be a tree whose roots are deep in the earth, but whose branches extend into heaven.

Bertrand Russell, English mathematician and philosopher,
1872–1970

Affection cannot be created; *it can only be liberated.*

Bertrand Russell, English mathematician and philosopher,
1872–1970

47

In love, assurances are practically an announcement of their opposite.

Elias Canetti, Austrian writer, 1903–1994

PEOPLE WHO SERVE YOU WITHOUT LOVE GET EVEN BEHIND YOUR BACK.

Walt Whitman, U.S. poet, 1819–1892

BRUTUS: Poor Brutus, with himself at war,
Forgets the shows of love to other men.

William Shakespeare, English playwright, 1564–1616
(Julius Caesar, *1599*)

IT is not love of self but hatred of self which is at the root of the troubles that afflict our world.

Eric Hoffer, U.S. longshoreman and writer, 1902–1983

Without self-love it is impossible to love others.

Hermann Hesse, German writer, 1877–1962

When love is suppressed, hate takes its place.

Havelock Ellis, English physician and psychologist, 1859–1939

Darkness cannot drive out darkness; only light can do that. Hate cannot drive out hate: only love can do that.

Martin Luther King Jr., U.S. clergyman and human rights leader, 1929–1968

FAME, WEALTH, AND HONOR! what are you to Love?

Alexander Pope, English poet, 1688–1744

WHERE LOVE REIGNS, there is no will to power; and where the will to power is paramount, *love is lacking.*

Carl G. Jung, Swiss psychiatrist, 1875–1961

When the power of love overcomes the love of power, the world will know peace.

Anonymous (U.S.), 1960s

Power said to the world, "You are mine."
The world kept it prisoner on her throne.
Love said to the world, "I am thine."
The world gave it the freedom of her
house.

Rabindranath Tagore, Indian poet,
1861–1941

We are most alive when we're in love.

John Updike, contemporary U.S. writer and critic

In love we discover the good qualities of our loved one which are hidden from other people.

Gerald Brenan, English writer, 1894–1987

WE are not loved because we are valued; we are valued because we are loved.

William Sloan Coffin, contemporary U.S. theologian

You are not loved when you are lovely, but when you are loved you are found to be lovely.

Ludwig Boerne, German writer, 1786–1837

"ALL YOU NEED IS LOVE."

John Lennon (1940-1980) and Paul McCartney (1942-), contemporary
English songwriters and singers (song title, 1967)

In the end the love you take is equal to the love you make.

John Lennon (1940-1980) and Paul McCartney (1942-), contemporary
English songwriters and singers (in the song "The End," 1967)

The love you give away is the only love you keep—*by benefiting*
another you benefit yourself.

Elbert Hubbard, U.S. writer and editor, 1856–1915

THERE IS IN THE HUMAN WILL AN

innate tendency, an inborn capacity for disinterested love. This power to love another for his own sake is one of the things that makes us like God.

Thomas Merton, U.S. monk and writer, 1915–1968

TRUE HAPPINESS IS FOUND IN UNSELFISH LOVE, A LOVE WHICH INCREASES IN PROPORTION AS IT IS SHARED.

Thomas Merton, U.S. monk and writer, 1915–1968

JACOB SERVED SEVEN years for Rachel, and they seemed to him but a few days because of the love he had for her.

Bible (Genesis 29:20)

MANY WATERS CANNOT QUENCH LOVE, NEITHER CAN FLOODS DROWN IT.

Bible (Song of Solomon 8:7)

Let your love be like the misty rain, coming softly, but flooding the river.

Madagascan Proverb

For this is love's truth: she joins two in one being, makes sweet sour, strangers neighbors, and the lowly noble.

Hadewijch of Brabant, Dutch poet, 1210–1280

What love is, if thou wouldst be taught,
Thy heart must teach alone
Two souls with but a single thought,
Two hearts that beat as one.

Friedrich Halm, German playwright, 1806–1871

*I*n love the paradox occurs that two beings become one and yet remain two.

Erich Fromm, German-born U.S. psychoanalyst, 1900–1980

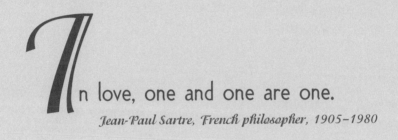

In love, one and one are one.

Jean-Paul Sartre, French philosopher, 1905–1980

WHEN we are not in love too much, we are not in love enough.

Comte de Bussy-Rabutin, French soldier and writer, 1618–1693

Iago: I humbly do beseech you of your pardon
For too much loving you.

William Shakespeare, English playwright, 1564–1616 (Othello, 1604)

TRUE LOVE IS like ghosts, which everyone talks about but few have seen.

François de La Rochefoucauld, French writer, 1613–1680

Love is the wisdom of the fool and *the folly of the wise.*

Samuel Johnson, English writer and lexicographer, 1709–1784

MUTUAL LOVE, THE CROWN OF ALL OUR BLISS.

John Milton, English poet, 1608–1674

I MET IN THE STREET a very poor young man who was in love. His hat was old, his coat was threadbare—there were holes at his elbows; the water passed through his shoes and the stars through his soul.

Victor Hugo, French writer, 1802–1885

LOVE IS A TYRANT, RESISTED.

John Ford, English playwright, 1586–1640

Give all to love;
Obey thy heart;
Friends, kindred, days,
Estate, good-fame,
Plans, credit and the Muse
Nothing refuse.

Ralph Waldo Emerson,
U.S. philosopher, 1803–1882

'TIS BETTER TO HAVE LOVED AND LOST
THAN NEVER TO HAVE LOVED AT ALL.

Alfred, Lord Tennyson, English poet, 1809–1892

To love and win is the best thing; to love and lose, the next best.

William Makepeace Thackeray, English writer, 1811–1863

IT IS BEST TO LOVE WISELY, NO DOUBT; but to love foolishly is better than not to be able to love at all.

William Makepeace Thackeray, English writer, 1811–1863

To be in love is to surpass oneself.
Oscar Wilde, English playwright, 1854–1900

LIKE EVERYBODY WHO IS NOT in love,
he imagined that one chose the person whom one loved after endless
deliberations and on the strength of various qualities and advantages.
Marcel Proust, French writer, 1871–1922

THE DESIRE TO GIVE inspires no affection unless there is also the power to withhold; and the successful wooer, in both sexes alike, is the one who can stand out for honorable conditions, and, failing them, *go without*.

George Bernard Shaw, British playwright and critic, 1856–1950

70

$\mathcal{L}$OVE is what happens to a man and a woman who don't know each other.

W. Somerset Maugham, English writer, 1874–1965

How can we love each other if we don't know each other? And how can we know each other if we don't love each other?

Julie Anne Bovasso, U.S. educator and playwright, 1930–1991

It is easier to fall in love when you are out of it than to get out of it when you are in.

François de La Rochefoucauld, French writer, 1613–1680

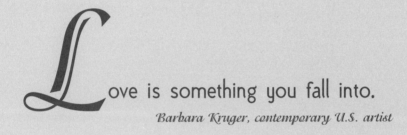

*L*ove is something you fall into.

Barbara Kruger, contemporary U.S. artist

My soul is crushed, my spirit sore
I do not like me anymore,
I cavil, quarrel, grumble, grouse
I ponder on the narrow house
I shudder at the thought of men
I'm due to fall in love again.

Dorothy Parker, U.S. writer
and humorist, 1893–1967

Life is a glorious cycle of song,
A medley of extemporania;
And love is a thing that can never
go wrong;
And I am Marie of Romania.

*Dorothy Parker, U.S. writer
and humorist, 1893–1967*

75

I WAS ABOUT HALF in love with her by the time we sat down. That's the thing about girls. Every time they do something pretty, even if they're not much to look at, or even if they are sort of stupid, you fall in love with them, and you never know where the hell you are.

J. D. Salinger, contemporary U.S. writer (in the novel The Catcher in the Rye, *1951)*

Love is much nicer to be in than an automobile accident, a tight girdle, a higher tax bracket or a holding pattern over Philadelphia.

Judith Viorst, contemporary U.S. writer

NOTHING TAKES THE TASTE OUT OF PEANUT BUTTER QUITE LIKE UNREQUITED LOVE.

Charles M. Schulz, U.S. cartoonist, 1922–2000 (Peanuts)

You need somebody to love you while you're looking for someone to love.

Shelagh Delaney, contemporary English playwright

In real love you want the other person's good. In romantic love you want *the other person.*

Margaret Anderson, U.S. writer and publisher, 1886–1973

77

WHAT PASSES AS LOVE between man and woman can be many things. Promiscuity, possessiveness, misuse of sex for purposes of power, are all highly disintegrative ... But love between man and woman that is the relationship in depth, the **"MARRIAGE OF TRUE MINDS,"** is a drawing to wholeness. Each calls up in the other the deep center, the seed of the Self. It is by such love that the **"REAL BEING"** grows and lives.

P. W. Martin, contemporary English psychologist

Love one another, but make not a bond of love:
Let it rather be a moving sea between the shores of your souls.
Kahlil Gibran, Syrian poet, 1883–1931

LOVE CONSISTS IN THIS, THAT TWO SOLITUDES
PROTECT AND TOUCH AND GREET EACH OTHER.
Rainer Maria Rilke, German poet, 1875–1926

Thinking of you, I break into bloom again.
Hsüeh Tao, Chinese poet and singer, 768–831

79

From their eyelids as they glanced
dripped love.

Hesiod, Greek poet, eighth century B.C.

80

At one glance
I love you
With a thousand hearts.

Mihri Hatun, Turkish poet, ?–1506

Oh, thou art fairer than the evening air
Clad in the beauty of a thousand stars.

*Christopher Marlowe, English playwright,
1564–1593*

Come live with me, and be my love,
And we will all the pleasures prove
That valleys, groves, hills, and fields,
Woods, or steepy mountain yields.

Christopher Marlowe, English playwright,
1564–1593

ROMEO: He jests at scars that never felt a wound.
[THEN JULIET APPEARS ABOVE AT A WINDOW]
But, soft! what light through yonder window breaks?
It is the east, and Juliet is the sun.

William Shakespeare, English playwright, 1564–1616
(Romeo and Juliet, *1594*)

JULIET: My bounty is as boundless as the sea,
My love as deep; the more I give to thee,
The more I have, for both are infinite.

William Shakespeare, English playwright, 1564–1616
(Romeo and Juliet, *1594*)

ROMEO: The brightness of her cheek would shame those stars,
As daylight doth a lamp; her eyes in heaven
Would through the airy region stream so bright
That birds would sing and think it were not night.
See, how she leans her cheek upon her hand!
O, that I were a glove upon that hand,
That I might touch that cheek!

William Shakespeare, English playwright, 1564–1616
(Romeo and Juliet, *1594*)

HAMLET: I loved Ophelia: forty thousand brothers
Could not, with all their quantity of love,
Make up my sum.

William Shakespeare, English playwright, 1564–1616
(Hamlet, *1600*)

Shall I compare thee to a summer's day?
Thou art more lovely and more temperate.

William Shakespeare, English playwright, 1564–1616
(Sonnets, 1609)

Thy sweet love remember'd such wealth brings
That then I scorn to change my state with kings.

William Shakespeare, English playwright, 1564–1616
(Sonnets, 1609)

Our state cannot be severed, we are one,
One flesh; to lose thee were to lose my self.

John Milton, English poet, 1608–1674

To love or not; in this we stand or fall.

John Milton, English poet, 1608–1674

O, my Luve is like a red, red rose,
That's newly sprung in June.
O, my Luve is like the melody,
That's sweetly played in tune.

Robert Burns, Scottish poet, 1759–1796

No riches from his scanty store
My love could impart;
He gave a boon I valued more—
He gave me all his heart.

Helen Maria Williams, English poet and writer, 1762–1827

I love your hills, and I love your dales,
And I love your flocks a-bleating—
But O, on the heather to lie together,
With both our hearts a-beating!

John Keats, English poet, 1795–1821

I made a garland for her head,
And bracelets too, and fragrant zone;
She looked at me as she did love,
And made sweet moan.

John Keats, English poet, 1795–1821

I loved him too as woman loves—
Reckless of sorrow, sin, or scorn.

*Letitia Elizabeth Landon, English poet and
writer, 1802–1838*

There be none of Beauty's daughters
With a magic like thee;
And like music on the waters
Is thy sweet voice to me.

Lord Byron, English poet, 1788–1824

How do I love thee?
Let me count the ways.
I love thee to the depth
and breadth and height
My soul can reach.

Elizabeth Barrett Browning,
English poet, 1806–1861

And stood by the rose-wreathed
gate. Alas,
We loved, sir—used to meet:
How sad and bad and mad it was—
But then, how it was sweet!

Robert Browning, English poet,
1812–1889

My heart is like a singing bird ...
The birthday of my life is come,
My love is come to me.

*Dante Gabriel Rossetti, English painter
and poet, 1828–1892*

She was a child and I was a child,
In this kingdom by the sea,
But we loved with a love that was
more than love—
I and my Annabel Lee.

*Edgar Allen Poe, U.S. poet and writer,
1809–1849 (in the poem "Annabel Lee,"
1849)*

I dream of Jeanie with the light brown hair,
Floating, like a vapor, on the soft summer air.

Stephen Foster, U.S. songwriter, 1828–1864 (in the song "Jeannie with the Light Brown Hair," 1854)

Beautiful dreamer, wake unto me,
Starlight and dewdrop are waiting for thee.

Stephen Foster, U.S. songwriter, 1828–1864 (in the song "Beautiful Dreamer," 1864)

Everything that touches us, me and you,
takes us together like a violin's bow,
which draws ONE voice out of two
separate strings.
Upon what instrument are we two
spanned?
And what musician holds us in his hand?

Rainer Maria Rilke, German poet, 1875–1926
(in the poem "Love Song")

Just because I loves you—
That's de reason why
Ma soul is full of color
Like da wings of a butterfly.

Langston Hughes, U.S. poet, 1902–1967
(in the poem "Reasons Why," 1922)

What is love? . . .
It is the morning and the evening star.

Sinclair Lewis, U.S. writer, 1885–1961
(in the novel Elmer Gantry, 1927)

Birds do it, bees do it,
Even educated fleas do it.
Let's do it, let's fall in love.

*Cole Porter, U.S. songwriter, 1891–1964
(in the song "Let's Do It," 1928)*

It's delightful, it's delicious, it's
de-lovely.

*Cole Porter, U.S. songwriter, 1891–1964
(in the song "It's De-Lovely," 1936)*

I can't give you anything but love, Baby,
That's the only thing I've plenty of, Baby.

*Dorothy Fields, U.S. songwriter, 1905–1974
(in the song "I Can't Give You Anything But
Love, Baby," 1928)*

Ain't misbehavin',
I'm savin' my love for you.

*Andy Razaf, U.S. songwriter, (1895–1973)
(in the song "Ain't Misbehavin'," 1929)*

Singin' in the rain, just singin' in the rain
What a glorious feeling, I'm happy again.

*Arthur Freed, U.S. songwriter and producer,
1894–1973 (in the song "Singin' in the Rain,"
1929)*

My funny Valentine, sweet comic Valentine,
You make me smile with my heart.

*Lorenz Hart, U.S. songwriter, 1896–1943
(in the song "My Funny Valentine" from
the musical Babes in Arms, 1937)*

Embrace me, my sweet embraceable you
Embrace me, you irreplaceable you.

Ira Gershwin, U.S. songwriter, 1896–1983
(in the song "Embraceable You" from the
musical Girl Crazy, *1930)*

I've got a crush on you, sweetie pie;
All the day and night times hear me sigh.

Ira Gershwin, U.S. songwriter, 1896–1983
(in the song "I've Got a Crush on You," 1930)

Night and day you are the one,
Only you beneath the moon and
under the sun.

*Cole Porter, U.S. songwriter, 1891–1964
(in the song "Night and Day," 1932)*

"I've Got You under My Skin."

*Cole Porter, U.S. songwriter, 1891–1964
(song title, 1936)*

But did thee feel the earth move?

*Ernest Hemingway, U.S. writer, 1899–1961
(in the novel* For Whom the Bell Tolls, *1940)*

Of all the gin joints in all the towns
in all the world, she walks into mine!

*Julius J. Epstein 1909–2000, Philip G.
Epstein 1909–1952, and Howard Koch
1902–1995, contemporary U.S. screenwriters
(spoken by Humphrey Bogart about Ingrid
Bergman in the film* Casablanca, *1942)*

107

Here's looking at you, kid.

Julius J. Epstein 1909–2000, Philip G. Epstein 1909–1952, and Howard Koch 1902–1995, U.S. screenwriters (farewell words spoken by Humphrey Bogart to Ingrid Bergman in the film Casablanca, 1942)

*Y*ou know how to whistle, don't you, Steve? You just put your lips together and blow.

William Faulkner, 1897–1962 and Jules Furthman, 1888–1966, U.S. writers, (spoken by Lauren Becall to Humphrey Bogart in To Have and Have Not, *1944)*

They say falling in love is wonderful,
It's wonderful, so they say.

Irving Berlin, Russian-born U.S. songwriter,
1888–1989 (in the song "Falling in Love"
from the musical Annie Get Your Gun, *1946)*

Some enchanted evening,
You may see a stranger,
You may see a stranger,
Across a crowded room.

Oscar Hammerstein II, U.S. songwriter, 1895–1960 (in the song "Some Enchanted Evening" from the musical South Pacific, 1949)

Love me tender, love me sweet,
Never let me go.

*Elvis Presley, U.S. singer,
1935–1977, and Vera Matson, contemporary U.S. songwriter (in the
song "Love Me Tender," 1956)*

C'mon, baby, light my fire
Try to set the night on fire.

*Jim Morrison and Robby Krieger,
contemporary U.S. songwriters (in
the song "Light My Fire," 1967)*

Eight days a week I love you.
John Lennon, (1940–1980) and Paul McCartney, (1942–) contemporary
English songwriters and singers (in the song "Eight Days a Week," 1964)

"Baby, You're the Only Dream I've Ever Had That's Come True."
Robert Duvall, contemporary U.S. actor (song title in the film Tender
Mercies, *1983)*

THE SLOWEST KISS MAKES TOO MUCH HASTE.
Thomas Middleton, English playwright, 1580–1627

CLOWN: What's to come is still unsure:
In delay there lies no plenty;
Then come kiss me, sweet and twenty,
Youth's a stuff will not endure.

*William Shakespeare, English playwright,
1564–1616 (Twelfth Night, 1601)*

And the sunlight clasps the earth
And the moonbeams kiss the sea:
What is all this sweet work worth
If thou kiss not me?

Percy Bysshe Shelley, English poet,
1792–1822

A long, long kiss, a kiss of youth, and love,
And beauty, all concentrating like rays
Into one focus, kindled from above.
Such kisses as belong to early days,
Where heart, and soul, and sense, in concert
move,
And the blood's lava, and the pulse ablaze,
Each kiss a heart-quake—for a kiss's strength,
I think it must be reckon'd by its length.

Lord Byron, English poet, 1788–1824

'Twas not into my ear you whispered, but into my heart.
'Twas not my lips you kissed, but my soul.

Judy Garland, U.S. actor, 1922–1969 (in the song "My Love Is Lost," 1939)

These two
Imparadis'd in one another's arms.

John Milton, English poet, 1608–1674

NO ACT CAN BE QUITE SO intimate as the sexual embrace. In its accomplishment, for all who have reached a reasonably human degree of development, the communion of bodies becomes the communion of souls. The outward and visible sign has been the consummation of an inward and spiritual grace.

Havelock Ellis, English physician and psychologist, 1859–1939

ROMANTIC LOVE IS SEXUALLY PASSIONATE LOVE. Romance uses sexual intimacy to create or amplify closeness and mutual fulfillment.

Peter R. Breggin, contemporary U.S. psychiatrist

You mustn't force sex to do the work of love or love to do the work of sex.

Mary McCarthy, U.S. writer and critic, 1912–1989

Where there's marriage without love, there will be love without marriage.

Anonymous

SPONTANEITY [IN LOVE-MAKING]

is everything ... sexual converse ought to proceed like verbal converse with mutual give and take.

Gerald Brenan, English writer, 1894–1987

Sex is a conversation carried out by other means.
Peter Ustinov, contemporary English actor and playwright

The highest level of sexual excitement is in a monogamous relationship.
Warren Beatty, contemporary U.S. actor

The absolute yearning of one human body for another particular one and its indifference to substitutes is one of life's major mysteries.

Iris Murdoch, Irish writer, 1919–1999

I THOUGHT WELL AS well him as another and then I asked him with my eyes to ask again yes and then he asked me would I yes to say yes my mountain flower and first I put my arms around him yes and drew him down to me so he could feel my breasts all perfume yes and his heart was going like mad and yes I said yes I will Yes.

James Joyce, Irish writer, 1882–1941 (last sentence of Ulysses, *1922)*

121

Breathes there a man
with soul so dead,
Who never to his
wife hath said,
Breakfast be damned,
come back to bed!

Anonymous

Folks, I'm telling you,
birthing is hard
and dying is mean—
so get yourself
a little loving
in between.

Langston Hughes,
U.S. poet, 1902–1967

123

IT AIN'T BECAUSE lovers are so sensitive that they quarrel so often; it is because there is so much fun in making up.

Josh Billings, U.S. writer and humorist, 1818–1885

I think our young people are getting it all together. Not that I think you should be making love all the time—who can do it all the time? *Though I do try.*

Cary Grant, English-born U.S. actor, 1904–1986

Love is the chain whereby to bind a child to its parents.

Abraham Lincoln, U.S. president, 1809–1865

124

It didn't take elaborate experiments to deduce that an infant would die from want of food. But it took centuries to figure out that infants can and do perish from want of love.

Louise J. Kaplan, contemporary U.S. psychologist

WE NEVER KNOW THE LOVE OF OUR PARENTS FOR US TILL WE HAVE BECOME PARENTS.

Henry Ward Beecher, U.S. clergyman, 1813–1887

The roots of a child's ability to cope and thrive, regardless of circumstance, lie in that child's having had at least a small, safe place (an apartment? a room? a lap?) in which, in the companionship of a loving person, that child could discover that he or she was lovable and capable of loving in return.

Fred Rogers, U.S. children's television personality, 1928–2003

THE MORE LOVE YOU GIVE YOUR

children, the more love you are helping them to create inside them-
selves. Think of love as a basic right of your kids. Give it away
freely, and it will come back a thousand fold.

Stephanie Marston, contemporary U.S. psychotherapist

Nothing's better than a mother's love.

African Proverb

My dad took me to Paris for

the weekend. We had the most amazing time. On the plane back to London, he asked me, "Do you know why I took you to Paris—only you and me?" And I said, "Why?" And he said, "Because I wanted you to see Paris for the first time with a man who would always love you."

Gwyneth Paltrow, contemporary U.S. actor

Children are love made visible.

U.S. Proverb

127

YOU SHALL LOVE THE LORD your God

with all your heart, and with all your soul, and with all your mind. This is the great and first commandment. And a second is like it, You shall love your neighbor as yourself. On these two commandments depend all the law and the prophets.

Jesus, Hebrew founder of Christianity, first century A.D. (Matthew 22:37–40; combining the teachings of Moses in Deuteronomy 6:4 and Leviticus 19:18)

Do you love your Creator? Love your fellow-beings first.

Muhammad, Arab founder of Islam, A.D. 570–632

128

Do not waste time bothering whether you **"LOVE"** your neighbor; act as if you did. As soon as we do this we find one of the great secrets. When you are behaving as if you loved someone, you will presently come to love him. If you injure someone you dislike, you will find yourself disliking him more. If you do him a good turn, you will find yourself disliking him less.

C. S. Lewis, English writer, 1898–1963

TO LOVE ONE'S SELF IN THE RIGHT WAY AND TO LOVE ONE'S NEIGHBOR ARE ABSOLUTELY ANALOGOUS CONCEPTS, ARE AT BOTTOM ONE AND THE SAME.

Søren Kierkegaard, Danish philosopher, 1813–1855

You have heard that it was said, **"YOU SHALL LOVE YOUR NEIGHBOR AND HATE YOUR ENEMY."** But I say to you, love your enemies and pray for those who persecute you, so that you may be sons of your Father who is in heaven.

Jesus, Hebrew founder of Christianity, first century A.D.
(Matthew 5:43–45)

Love is the only force capable of transforming an enemy into a friend.

Martin Luther King Jr., U.S. clergyman and human rights leader,
1929–1968

IF I SPEAK IN THE TONGUES OF

men and of angels, but have not love, I am a noisy gong or a clanging cymbal. And if I have prophetic powers, and understand all mysteries and all knowledge, and if I have all faith, so as to remove mountains, but have not love, I am nothing.

Paul, Christian apostle, first century A.D. (1 Corinthians 13:1–2)

It is love, not faith, that removes mountains.
George Sand (Armandine-Aurore-Lucile Dudevant), French writer,
1804–1876

LOVE IS PATIENT AND KIND; love is

not jealous or boastful; it is not arrogant or rude. Love does not insist on its own way; it is not irritable or resentful; it does not rejoice at wrong, but rejoices in the right. Love bears all things, believes all things, hopes all things, endures all things.

Paul, Christian apostle, first century A.D. (1 Corinthians 13:4–7)

So faith, hope, love abide, these three; *but the greatest of these is love.*

Paul, Christian apostle, first century A.D. (1 Corinthians 13:13)

132

It is love, then, that you should strive for.

Paul, Christian apostle, first century A.D. (1 Corinthians 14:1)

Our love should not be just words and talk; it must be true love, which shows itself in action.

John, Christian apostle, first century A.D. (1 John 3:18)

LET US LOVE ONE ANOTHER; for love is of God, and he who loves is born of God and knows God. He who does not love does not know God; for God is love.

John, Christian apostle, first century A.D. (1 John 4:8)

WE LOVE BECAUSE GOD FIRST LOVED US. If someone says he loves God, but hates his brother, he is a liar. For he cannot love God, whom he has not seen, if he does not love his brother, whom he has seen. The command that Christ has given us is this: whoever loves God must love his brother also.

John, Christian apostle, first century A.D. (1 John 4:19–21)

Who have all the powers of their soul in harmony, and the same loving mind for all; who find joy in the good of all beings—*they reach in truth my very self.*

Bhagavad Gita, Hindu scriptures, sixth century B.C.

I commune with my heart in the night;
I meditate and search my spirit:
"Will the Lord spurn for ever,
and never again be favorable?
Has His steadfast love for ever ceased?
Are His promises at an end for all time?
Has God forgotten to be gracious?
Has He in anger shut up his compassion?"

Bible (Psalms 77:6–9)

In overflowing wrath for a moment
I hid my face from you,
but with everlasting love
I will have compassion on you,
says the Lord, your Redeemer.

Isaiah, Hebrew prophet, eighth century B.C.
(Isaiah 54:8)

GOD loves each one of us as if there were only one of us to love.

St. Augustine, Christian theologian, fifth century A.D.

Knowing God and loving God are identical.

Moses Maimonides, Jewish physician and philosopher, 1135–1204

O divine Master, grant that I may not
so much seek
To be consoled as to console;
To be understood as to understand;
To be loved as to love.
For it is in giving that we receive;
It is in pardoning that we are pardoned;
And it is in dying that we are born to
eternal life.

*St. Francis of Assisi, Italian monk and
founder of the Franciscan Order, 1181–1226
("The Prayer of St. Francis")*

LOVE IS A MIGHTY POWER, a great and complete good. Love alone lightens every burden, and makes the rough places smooth ... Nothing is sweeter than love, nothing stronger, nothing higher, nothing wider, nothing more pleasant, nothing fuller or better in heaven or earth; for love is born of God, and can rest only in God, above all created things.

Love flies, runs, and leaps for joy; it is free and unrestrained. Love gives all for all, resting in One who is highest above all things, from whom every good flows and proceeds. Love does not regard the gifts, but turns to the Giver of all gifts.

Thomas à Kempis, German monk, 1380–1471

NATURE HATH IMPLANTED IN OUR

breasts a love of others, a sense of duty to them, a moral instinct, in short, which prompts us irresistibly to feel and to succor their distresses. . . . The Creator would indeed have been a bungling artist had he intended man for a social animal without planting in him social dispositions.

Thomas Jefferson, U.S. president, 1743–1826

Would that I could love the best of men as tenderly as God loves the worst.

Anonymous (Hasidic)

ANONYMOUS FATHER: My son has forsaken God. What, Rabbi, shall I do?
BAAL SHEM TOV: Love him more than ever.

Baal Shem Tov, Jewish religious leader and founder of Hasidism,
1690–1760

Love a man even in his sin, for that is the semblance of Divine Love and is the highest love on earth. Love all God's creation, the whole and every grain of sand of it. Love every leaf, every ray of God's light. Love the animals, love the plants, love everything. **IF YOU LOVE EVERYTHING, YOU WILL PERCEIVE THE DIVINE MYSTERY IN THINGS.**

Fyodor Dostoyevsky, Russian writer, 1821–1881

Those who love God love everyone.
Gottfried Leibniz, German philosopher and mathematician, 1646–1716

When you love you should not say, "God is in my heart," but rather, "I am in the heart of God." And think not you can direct the course of love, for love, if it finds you worthy, directs your course.

Kahlil Gibran, Syrian poet, 1883–1931

God needs us, just as we need God. Why should He need us unless it be to love us? . . . [IN THIS VIEW, CREATION IS] God undertaking to create creators, that He may have, besides Himself, beings worthy of His love.

Henri Bergson, French philosopher, 1859–1941

IT IS ONLY through love that we can attain to communion with God. All living knowledge of God rests upon this foundation: that we experience Him in our lives as Will-to-Love.

Albert Schweitzer, German physician and theologian, 1875–1965

WHERE LOVE IS, THERE GOD IS ALSO.

Mohandas K. Gandhi, Indian spiritual and nationalist leader,
1869–1948

God's love is unlimited but . . . *his power is not.*

Arnold J. Toynbee, English historian, 1889–1975

I think I have discovered the highest good. *It is love.* This principle stands at the center of the cosmos. As John says, "God is love." He who loves is a participant in the being of God. He who hates does not know God.

Martin Luther King Jr., U.S. clergyman and human rights leader,
1929–1968

NO MERE EFFORT OF OURS CAN MAKE OUR LOVE PERFECT. THE PEACE, CERTITUDE, LIBERTY, FEARLESSNESS OF PURE LOVE, ARE GIFTS OF GOD.

Thomas Merton, U.S. monk and writer, 1915–1968

LIFE IS SO PRECIOUS. Please, please, let's love one another, live each day, reach out to each other, be kind to each other. Peace be with you. God is great.

Julia Roberts, contemporary U.S. actor (closing words of her talk at a nationally televised benefit for the September 11 victims and their families, September 21, 2001)

Children of the future Age
Reading this indignant page,
Know that in a former time,
Love! sweet Love! was thought a crime.

William Blake, English poet and painter,
1757–1827

Love to faults is always blind,
Always is to joy inclin'd,
Lawless, wing'd, and unconfin'd,
And breaks all chains from every mind.

William Blake, English poet and painter,
1757–1827

146

While over Alabama earth
These words are gently spoken
Serve—and hate will die unborn
Love—and chains are broken.

Langston Hughes, U.S. poet, 1902–1967

147

REVOLUTIONARY LOVE INVOLVES
putting into action the laws of the Kingdom before the Kingdom has really come.

American Friends Service Committee (in the pamphlet "Speak Truth to Power," 1955)

Unarmed love is the most powerful force in all the world.

Martin Luther King Jr., U.S. clergyman and human rights leader, 1929–1968

An army of lovers shall not fail.

Rita Mae Brown, contemporary U.S. writer and poet

*T*HE fulcrum has yet to be found that shall enable the lever of love to move the world.

Charles Sanders Peirce, U.S. philosopher, 1839–1914

"Love, the Answer to the Problem of Human Existence."

Erich Fromm, German-born U.S. psychoanalyst, 1900–1980
(chapter title from his book The Art of Loving, *1956)*

LOVE IS THE FINAL END OF THE WORLD'S HISTORY,
THE AMEN OF THE UNIVERSE.

Novalis, German poet, 1772–1801

THE FIRST HOPE in our inventory—the hope that
includes and at the same time transcends all others—must be the
hope that love is going to have the last word.

Arnold J. Toynbee, English historian, 1889–1975

I REFUSE TO ACCEPT THE cynical notion that nation after nation must spiral down a militaristic stairway into the hell of thermonuclear destruction. I believe that unarmed truth and unconditional love will have the final word in reality.

Martin Luther King Jr., U.S. clergyman and human rights leader, 1929–1968 (Nobel Peace Prize acceptance address, Oslo, Norway, December 11, 1964)

LEONARD ROY FRANK, a native of Brooklyn, graduated from the Wharton School of the University of Pennsylvania in 1954. A resident of San Francisco, he managed his own art gallery in the 1970s and has edited a number of books, including *Random House Webster's Quotationary* and *Freedom*. His e-mail address is **lfrank@igc.org**

152